LEVEL SIX
(F or Gr. 4)

JOHN W. SCHAUM *Presents*

Wedding Music

For Piano, Organ or Electronic Keyboard

FOREWORD

THIS album of Wedding Music contains "something old, something new, something borrowed" — but nothing blue. The compilation includes the all-time favorites plus several new additions to the wedding repertoire. For example the "American Wedding March" by Rudolf Friml is a stirring number. The "Wedding March" by Richard Hoffman is stately and dignified. Saint-Saens' "Benediction Nuptiale" is a sensitive composition suitable for the service. The book includes music for all phases of the wedding.

Although the contents are divided into different classifications most of the pieces may be interchanged for other categories and are not essentially restricted to the one indicated. The music is appropriate wherever the wedding takes place, whether in church, at home or in a private or public hall.

John W. Schaum

SCHAUM PUBLICATIONS, INC.
10235 N. Port Washington Rd. • Mequon, WI 53092
www.schaumpiano.net

06-70
CT-14

Classified Index

PRE-NUPTIAL RECITAL MUSIC

PROCESSIONAL MUSIC

RECESSIONAL MUSIC

WEDDING CEREMONY MUSIC

RECEPTION MUSIC

Alphabetical Index

Note: for additional wedding music, the book "Romantic Cameos" by John W. Schaum is recommended. It contains distinctive piano transcriptions of *Love's Old Sweet Song; Melody of Love; Schubert's Serenade; I Love Thee* by Grieg, etc.

Theme from "Water Music"

G. F. Handel (1685-1759)
Arr. by John W. Schaum

Larghetto M. M. ♩. = 50–60

Sinfonia from "Wedding Cantata"

J. S. Bach (1685 - 1750)
Freely Paraphrased by John W. Schaum

Andante M. M. ♩ = 84–96

mf
f
ff molto rit.
fz

Psalm Nineteen

Benedetto Marcello (1686-1739)
Arr. by John W. Schaum

Andantino M. M. ♩=74–96

p
f
p
f
p
rit.
f

Wedding March

Richard Hoffman (1831-1909)
Arr. by John W. Schaum

Maestoso M. M. ♩= 104–116

Ode to Joy

(From the Ninth Symphony)

Ludvig Van Beethoven (1770-1827)
Arr. by John W. Schaum

Giocoso M. M. ♩ = 96–112

Bridal Chorus

from "Lohengrin"

Richard Wagner (1813-1883)
Arr. by John W. Schaum

Trumpet Voluntary in D

Henry Purcell (1658-1695)
Arr. by John W. Schaum

Maestoso M. M. ♩=72–84

Impatience

F. Schubert (1797-1828)
Arr. by John W. Schaum

f
mf
p

Prayer from "Suite Gothique"

L. Boellmann (1862-1897)
Arr. by John W. Schaum

Lento M. M. ♩ = 120 – 132

Animato
mf
f
mf
a tempo
p
rit.
pp
mf
pp
ritard.

Because

Guy d' Hardelot (1858-1936)
Arr. by John W. Schaum

I am led through tears and joy to thee, Be - cause
agitato
you speak to me. Be - cause God made thee
p
espressivo
mine I'll cher - ish thee, Through light and
dark - ness, through all time to be, And pray His love may make our love di -
vine, Be - cause God made thee mine.
mf
rit.
p

I Love You Truly

Carrie Jacobs-Bond (1862-1946)
Arr. by John W. Schaum

Allegretto M. M. ♩=96–112

Calm as the Night

Lyrics by J. W. S.

Carl Bohm (1844-1920)

Arr. by John W. Schaum

Comodo M. M. ♩=112–126

O Promise Me

Op. 50

Clement Scott

R. De Koven (1859-1920)
Arr. by John W. Schaum

Allegro M.M. ♩= 112–132

Spring Song

Alfred Hollins (1865-1942)
Arr. by John W. Schaum

p
mf
mf
p
mf
p
rit.

Traumerei

R. Schumann (1810-1856)
Arr. by John W. Schaum

Lord Bless You

Peter C. Lutkin (1858-1931)
Arr. by John W. Schaum

O Perfect Love

Joseph Barnby (1838-1896)
Arr. by John W. Schaum

Lento M. M. ♩= 92–104

Benediction Nuptiale

(Op. 9)

C. Saint-Saens (1835-1921)
Arr. by John W. Schaum

mf
f
rit.
p a tempo
pp sotto voce
rit.

Wedding March

from "MIDSUMMER NIGHT'S DREAM"

Felix Mendelssohn (1809-1847)
Arr. by John W. Schaum

Con moto M. M. ♩= 104–116

ff
mf
ff
mf
ff
D. S. optional

American Wedding March

Rudolf Friml
Arr. by John W. Schaum

sotto voce
mp
ten.
f
ff
ten.
p dolce

rit.
ff
ten.